ALL VIENNA

Text: Carlos de Haro.

Photographs: Miguel Raurich and Photographic Archives of FISA-Escudo de Oro.

Diagrams and reproduction conceived and carried
out in their entirety by the technical teams of
EDITORIAL FISA ESCUDO DE ORO, S.A.

ESCUDO DE ORO

Vienna, the Austrian capital, sits on the banks of the Danube, right at the foot of the last slopes of the Alps and is surrounded by that large green belt made up by the so-called Vienna Woods. The cultural, political and economic heart of the country, the city is divided into 23 municipal districts, known as *bezirke*, the first of which encompasses the oldest part of town, the so-called *Innere Stadt* or inner city. It has a population of slightly over 1.6 million inhabitants and stretches over 415 square kilometres. The winters are cold and humid, while the summers tend to be pleasantly mild. Life in what was once the capital of one of the most powerful 19th century empires unfurls at the pace of a slow waltz. Some of the greatest composers in history, such as Strauss, Mozart, Beethoven and Schubert, were born or raised here. Their music still echoes amid the walls of its sumptuous palaces, its large parks and avenues, and its cosy cafés. Vienna is also the city where Sigmund Freud, Otto Wagner and Gustav Klimt revolutionised the fields of psychology, architecture and painting, respectively, offering one more example of the traditional and extraordinary cultural vitality of which Vienna has always prided itself. At the same time it is the city of lively flea markets and up-end fashion stores, of Sachertorte and select pastry shops, of the Hapsburg and

THE VIEW FROM THE 150-METER-HIGH VIEWPOINT AT THE DANUBE TOWER, LOOKING TOWARD THE "ALTE DONAU" OR OLD DANUBE AND THE NORTH-EASTERN PART OF THE CITY.

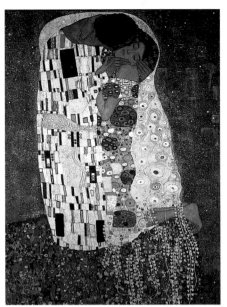

"THE KISS," BY GUSTAV KLIMT, ON DISPLAY AT THE BELVEDERE MUSEUM.

THE KINSKY PALACE, WITH ITS BAROQUE FAÇADE, IS A MASTERPIECE BY HILDEBRANDT (AT 4 FREYUNG, IN THE CITY CENTRE).

LEOPOLD CHURCH (KIRCHE AM STEINHOF), DESIGNED BY OTTO WAGNER IN 1905-07 (AT 1, BAUMGARTNER HÖHE, PENZING DISTRICT).

THE CONCERT HALL (KONZERTHAUS) AND THE THEATRE ACADEMY (THEATERAKADEMIE) NEXT TO LOTHRINGERSTRASSE.

the headquarters of different international organizations. In sum, Vienna is a fascinating and open city and visitors will easily fall under the spell of any of its wide-ranging charms.

MOZART'S FIGURE IS EVER-PRESENT IN THE CITY; HERE THE COMPOSER PORTRAYED ON A HOT AIR BALLOON IN THE VOLKSGARTEN.

AT THE INTERACTIVE EXHIBITION AT THE "HAUS DER MUSIK" VISITORS CAN EXPERIMENT WITH SOUND AND MUSIC (30, SEILERSTÄTTE, IN THE CITY CENTRE).

TRADITIONAL MUSIC BAND AT THE MUSEUMSQUARTIER.

In the first century, right on the spot where around the year 400 BC sat a Celtic settlement, the Romans established a garrison not far from an older one known as Carnuntum. It was not long before this new hamlet called Vindobona or white city, had acquired great strategic value for the Roman Empire in its wars against the

FLEA MARKET AT THE SQUARE FACING THE SCOTTISH MONASTERY.

A VIEW OF THE FLOHMARKT, THE POPULAR SECOND-HAND FLEA MARKET THAT TAKES PLACE EVERY SATURDAY NEXT TO THE NASCHMARKT.

IN THE CITY CENTRE, BEAUTIFUL PALACES TODAY HOUSE ELEGANT STORES.

AT ANY CORNER IN VIENNA VISITORS CAN SHARE A TABLE AND HAVE A DRINK; HERE, THE SMALL SQUARE NEXT TO ST. RUPERT'S CHURCH.

Germanic tribes. In one of those battles that took place around that time Emperor Marcus Aurelius was killed. It was the year 180 AD.

The city was destroyed by the Visigoths in 400 AD and conquered by Charlemagne in the ninth century. The Babengerg Dynasty took control of the Eastern March of the Holy Roman Empire (Ostmark), which would become the embryo of the future Austria, in 976. In

COFFEE WITH WHIPPED CREAM AND SACHERTORTE.

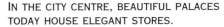

A VIENNA CLASSIC: THE CENTRAL CAFÉ, AT 14, HERRENGASSE, IN THE CITY CENTRE.

THE LARGE ROMAN CORNERSTONE ("RÖMISCHE RIESENQUADERN") FROM THE OLD VINDOBONA (AT 3, STERNGASSE, IN THE CITY CENTRE).

"VIENNA, SEEN FROM THE BELVEDERE," PAINTING BY BERNARDO BELLOTTO, 1759.

1137 Vienna was awarded city status and in 1156 it became the capital of the Duchy, the new name for the old Ostmark.

SCHÖNBRUNN: GARDENS, IMPERIAL PALACE AND TOURIST CARRIAGE.

In the late 13th century, the Babenberg Dynasty disappeared and the Hapsburg entered the scene. One of them, Ferdinand I, decided in 1521 to move the capital of the Holy Roman Empire to Vienna, a decision that would become a cornerstone in the city's history. Only eight years later, the recently established capital had to withstand the siege of the Turks, who would attack it again in 1683. In the 18th century Vienna witnessed an age of splendour epitomised by the blossoming of baroque art and culture and the construction of emblematic buildings such as the Schönbrunn. Another key moment for Vienna would arrive in 1857. On that year, Franz Joseph I signed a decree to tear down the old medieval walls, giving way to an ambitious urban development plan that would transform Vienna into an elegant and modern capital. This was a time of progress in all spheres –including economic, cultural and demographic development– and of constant social and artistic innovation. In this context of prosperity emerged one of

THE UNUSUAL METAL FAÇADE OF ZENTRALPARKASSE (CENTRAL SAVINGS BANK) AT 118, FAVORITENSTRASSE, IN DISTRICT 10, BY ARCHITECT GÜNTHER DOMENIG, DATING FROM 1975-79.

the most popular characters in Austrian history, Sissi, brought back to life 100 years later in the three films starring the Viennese actress Romy Schneider. Elizabeth, Princess of Bavaria, married at 17, in 1854, Emperor Franz Joseph I. Cultivated, curious, somewhat rebellious and uncomfortable amid the strict protocol of the royal Court, Sissi was murdered in 1898, at 61 years of age, in Geneva by an anarchist.
The Austro-Hungarian Empire dis-appeared after the death of Emperor Franz Joseph I in 1916 and with the proclamation of the republic in 1918 after the end of World War First. With it vanished the dreams of grandeur of the Hapsburg. After it was annexed by Nazi Germany in 1938 and later occupied by the victorious Allied powers after World War Second, Austria recovered its independence in 1955, and with it resurged Vienna's conciliating and creative spirit.

ONE LEVEL OF THE REICHSBRÜCKE BRIDGE OVER THE DANUBE IS RESERVED FOR PEDESTRIANS AND CYCLISTS. IN THE BACKGROUND THE UNO CITY.

A VIEW OF VIENNA FROM THE CATHEDRAL'S ROOF.

Sitting in the heart of old Vienna, in the very centre of town, **St. Stephen's Cathedral** (Stephansdom) is the most emblematic building of the Austrian capital, its true symbol. This wonderful exponent of the country's Gothic architecture presides over **St. Stephen's Square** (Stephansplatz), which until well into the 18th century used to be a cemetery. The origins of the temple date back to the 12th century, specifically to 1137, which is when the building work on a small Romanesque church was completed. The latter would be virtually destroyed to the ground by a fire in 1258. Almost completely rebuilt by 1263, the cathedral started to acquire its current appearance in 1304, which is when a large remodelling project took off already under the influence of Gothic art. Although these works would end in the middle of the 15th century, the building would still undergo some later architectural transformations. In the 16th century, for instance, the North Tower was capped by a renaissance-styled dome, and a spectacular pulpit by the cathedral's master craftsman, Anton Pilgram, was set up.

The appeal of this monumental temple financed by the Babenberg and finished by the Hapsburg is varied. Of its primitive Romanesque style remains, for instance, the Giants' Door (Riesentor) and the Towers of the Pagans, which are 65 meters tall. Taller still is the South Tower, rising 136 meters into the sky, which was erected between 1363 and 1433. Popularly known as Steffl Tower (small Stephen,) it has a viewpoint that offers a wonderful panoramic view of Vienna and that can be reached via a staircase with 343 steps. The North

ST.
STEPHEN'S
CATHEDRAL.

THE CATHEDRAL'S APSE: IMAGE OF ST. JOHN CAPRISTAN.

Tower is only 68 meters tall. Its construction was, according to some sources, interrupted in the early 16th century for aesthetic reasons, while others argue that it was cut short because of budget constraints. The debate was finally closed in 1579 with the construction of a beautiful Renaissance dome over it. Also particularly striking from the outside are the 230,000 enamelled roof tiles, placed in 1952 as part of the repair works to restore the parts of the cathedral damaged in World War Second. To a large extent the cathedral's restoration was made possible by the anonymous donations made by thousands of Austrians eager to see the past splendour of their historic buildings restored. These contributions also helped to recast the Pummerin Bell, destroyed in 1945 and very much loved by the Viennese people who rally to Stephansplatz every December 31 to hear the bells greet the New Year.

The interior is divided into three naves, each 107 meters long and separated from each other by

ROOF TILES. THE COATS OF ARMS WERE RESTORED AFTER THE DAMAGE THEY SUFFERED DURING WORLD WAR SECOND.

THE PUMMERIN BELL.

12, three-meter-wide columns. In the main nave you will find one of the cathedral's main attractions; a wonderful late Gothic pulpit carved in 1515 by master Anton Pilgram. On it are the images of the four Doctors of the Latin Church (St. Jerome, St. Au-

ANTON PILGRAM'S PULPIT.

"FENSTERGUCKER" ("THE MAN WHO LEANS OUT THE WINDOW"), AT THE BOTTOM OF THE PULPIT, IS A SELF-PORTRAIT OF MASTER ANTON PILGRAM.

THE CENTRAL NAVE.

THE HIGH ALTAR.

gustine, St. Gregory and St. Ambrose), as well as various toads and lizards that represent evil. On the base of the pulpit, as if he were looking out a window, is the face of Anton Pilgram himself. There is another self-portrait of the cathedral's old master craftsman in the left nave.

The Gothic statue of the Servants' Madonna, dating from 1320, is another of the cathedral's most prized works of art. Apparently, the image was donated to the cathedral by a noble Viennese woman who had unfairly accused one of her servants of stealing from her. Also worth noting is the temple's high altar presided by a large painting representing St Stephen's dilapidation.

In the right nave is the tomb of Emperor Frederic III, made of red marble, and in the left nave is the altar to the new city of Vienna (Wiener Neustädter Altar). Engraved on the later is Frederic III's motto — AEIOU, the meaning of which has not yet been deciphered today. In this same nave is buried Prince Eugene of Savoy. It is also

MADONNA OF THE SERVANTS.

15

MADONNA OF THE PROTECTIVE MANTLE (1450-1500).

EIGHTH CENTURY FIGURE OF THE SACRED HEART.

possible to visit the many crypts built under the cathedral, in which rest the remains of some of the members of the Hapsburg Dynasty. But aside from history lovers, music lovers will also find a reason to try to find out more about this wonderful temple, as it was here where the great composer Wolfgang Amadeus Mozart mar-

SEPULCHRE OF EMPEROR FREDERIC III.

ried Constanze Weber in 1782 and the place where nine years later his funeral mass was held.

A main meeting point for Vienna's dwellers, Stephenplatz has more to offer. Among other things are the remains of **St. Virgil's Chapel (Virgilkapelle),** discovered during building works in the subway and that today form part of a museum. The entrance to the museum is actually located in the subway station itself. It is possible to make out the dimensions and the exact location of this 13th century chapel thanks to the outline of it drawn on the pavement.

On one of the sides of the square, almost across from the cathedral, is **Haas House (Haas-Haus).** This contemporary building, dating from 1990, replaced a 19th century warehouse damaged at the end of World War Second. Its avantgarde design by Hans Hollein was very controversial, criticized for clashing with the square's main aes-

STOCK IM EISEN.

HAAS HOUSE.

thetic line. Its glass, curved façade is one of its most outstanding elements, and on it reflects the cathedral's silhouette. The cafeteria's outdoor sitting area provides the always appealing option of leisurely admiring the temple and the square's beauty.

On the corner with Kärtner Strasse, inside a small niche carved into a wall and well locked is an old piece of holm oak wood. It is the **Stock im Eisen (staff in iron).** According to the legend, all locksmiths admitted into the Vienna guild had to hammer a nail into it.

FOUNTAIN OF THE ESPOUSALS.

The deepest roots of the Austrian capital can be found in the inner city (Innere Stadt), that is, in the area of Vienna stretching from Donaukanal to Ringstrasse. Some of its streets and squares still proudly boast elements of its Roman and Medieval past. It is the case of the **Hoher Markt (High Market),** one of the city's historical landmarks, as it stands in the oldest square of the city, which was the very heart of Vienna until the 12th century. Archaeologists found here the remains of Vindobona, the garrison –first just a secondary one and then the main one in the area– founded by the Roman legions in the first century to combat the Germanic tribes. The remains can be visited on 3, Hoher Markt Square. At the heart of the square is the **Fountain of the Betrothed (Vermählungsbrunnen),** which represents the wedding of St. Joseph and Virgin Mary. It was built in 1702, commissioned by Leopold I to fulfil his promise to do so if his son Joseph I came back alive from a military campaign. The first fountain was made of wood and was replaced by the current one, carved on marble and bronze and designed by Joseph Emanuel Fischer von Erlach, who worked on it from 1729 to 1732.

Another of Hoher Markt's peculiarities is the **Ankeruhr** clock, located between the building of the Anker insurance company, on numbers 10-11, and the house next door, number 12. An exponent of the so-called *Jugendstil* style, it was designed in 1913 by painter Franz von Matsch. On the hour, every hour, a different character parades out from it to the chime of different melodies. There are 12 characters, including Marcus Aurelius, Charlemagne, Maria Theresa and Prince Eugene of Savoy.

Nor far from Hoher Markt is the old **City Hall (Alte Rathaus)**, dating from the 15th century. The building housed the City Hall until 1883, when the new municipal headquarters were inaugurated in the Ringstrasse. Particularly interesting are its courtyard, with its 1741 Andromeda Fountain, and its early 18th century Baroque façade. Next to it is the **Maria am Gestade Church.** An excellent exponent of Gothic architecture, it was built be-

HOHER MARKT: A DETAIL OF THE ANKERUHR CLOCK, WHICH TELLS THE TIME WITH THE PARADE OF DIFFERENT CHARACTERS.

tween the 14th and 15th centuries to replace a previous, 12th century temple. Although it is very popular today, as it hosts the remains of St Clemens Maria, patron saint of Vienna, the Church has not always been that revered. In 1786 it was even secularized and came close to being torn down. After being used as a warehouse it was reconsecrated in 1812.

MARIA AM GESTADE CHURCH.

ST. RUPERT CHURCH.

JUDENPLATZ.

Also close to Hoher Markt is **St. Rupert's Church (Ruprechtskirche)**, the oldest in Vienna. It is believed to have been founded in 740 by the Salzburg diocese, to which Vienna was ascribed until the ninth century. The fact that St. Rupert was the first Bishop of Salzburg strengthens this hypothesis. The origins of the current church are placed in the year 1161. Particularly striking from the outside are the Romanesque façade and the tower, part of which dates back to the ninth century.

JEWISH MUSEUM AND SYNAGOGUE.

Inside it is possible to see a combination of Romanesque, Gothic and Renaissance elements.

The nearby **Judenplatz** Square is a compulsory pit stop for those who would like to find out about the fate of the Jews who have inhabited Vienna throughout history. At the **Misrachi House**, an exhibition offers a retrospective of the history of Judaism in the Middle Ages and another one documents the tragic fate of the 65,000 Viennese Jews who became victims of the Holocaust. On the same square is one of the branches of the **Jewish Museum (Jüdisches Museum)**, which traces the history of Jews in Vienna until 1421, while the **Memorial for the Shoah victims**, a 10 by seven and 3.8 meters tall, concrete block by Rachel Whiteread showcases the books of a shut down library and the names of the Nazi death camps where Austria's Jews died. Anoth-

THE CLOCKS MUSEUM.

er reference for local Jews is the 13th century **Synagogue** discovered between 1995 and 1998 on a nearby street that is also where the **Clocks Museum (Uhrenmuseum)** and the **Toys Museum (Puppen- und Spielzeugmuseum)** are located. The large building that towers over Judenplatz is the old **Bohemian Court Chancery (ehemalige Böhmische Hofkanzlei)**, built between

OLD BOHEMIAN CHANCERY.

AM HOF SQUARE: AM HOF CHURCH AND MARY COLUMN.

1708 and 1714, and that today houses the court of accounts.

Before the Hapsburg stepped into power, the Babenberg had been the ones in charge of the country from 976 and 1246. At the nearby **Am Hof,** which was at the central point of the old Roman garrison, is where the Babenberg built their palace, hence its name: Near the court. In what was once the palace's Romanesque chapel, the Carmelites erected between 1386 and 1403 the **Church of the Nine Choirs of the Angels (Kirche zu den neum Chören der Engel)**

THE INTERIOR OF THE AM HOF CHURCH.

or **Am Hof Church,** which in the 16th century was transferred to the Jesuits. A transformation in the early 17th century left on the temple the Baroque trademark that characterizes it. The church was a first-hand witness of several key historic events. In 1782 Pius VI rendered his *urbi et orbi* blessing from its balcony. In 1804, Franz I announced from it he would be crowned Emperor of Austria, and two years later, the end of the Holy Roman Empire.

Across from it rises the **Virgin Mary Column (Mariensäule),**

THE OLD ARMOURY.

dating from 1645. On it is depicted the battle of the angels and the four scours of humanity: Hunger, symbolised by a dragon, heresy, by a snake, the plague, by a basilisk, and war, by a lion.

Also in Am Hof is the **Old Armory (Alte Zeughaus)**, now a garrison and the Fire-fighters Museum. In the building's basement it is possible to see some of the few Roman remains to be found in Vienna. **Märklein House**, of 1730, stands on the grounds where the Babengerg Palace once was.

In the nearby Freyung Square is the **Scottish Monastery (Schottenkloster)**, which was given this name because it was founded in the 12th century by a group of Irish monks, then known as Scotia Maior. It houses the oldest image of the Virgin Mary in Vienna, dating back to the 13th century. It also houses an important painting collection that includes works by Rubens.

Next to he latter is the **Minorite Church (Minoritenkirche)**, dating from the 14th century, although it was rebuilt in the 18th century. This Gothic temple has changed

SCOTTISH MONASTERY.

MINORITE
CHURCH.

FERSTEL PALACE: COURTYARD AND GALLERY WITH ITS ELEGANT STORES.

hands several times. It was built by Franciscan monks, who in 1784 handed it over the Italian congregation of the Mary of the Snows, to then recover it again in 1957. In Herrengasse, behind the Ferstel Palace, it is difficult to miss the **Café Central**, the best known of Vienna's many and popular cafés. Since the first one opened its doors in 1685, cafés have not just become an essential element in Vienna's urban landscape but also symbolise a particular understanding of social life for generations of Vienna's dwellers. Savouring a cup of coffee in an elegant and serene café while enjoying one of those conversations that are free from the tyranny of time has been, and still is, almost a religion in the Austrian capital. Although throughout their history these establishments have been a traditional meeting point for intellectuals, artists and politicians, the truth is that here, they are frequented by almost everybody.

THE CENTRAL CAFÉ.

"GRABEN"; BEHIND THE TERRACES IS THE PLAGUE COLUMN.

ST. LEOPOLD III FOUNTAIN.

What is now perhaps Vienna's most elegant street was until the 12th century a ditch (graben) that marked the city's western limit. With time, this street of up-market stores and elegant cafés would become the stage for outdoor markets, tournaments and ceremonies. It started becoming one of the capital's main arteries in the 18th century, under the rule of Maria Theresa. Some years earlier, in 1687, Leopold I had ordered the building of a monument in tribute to the Holy Trinity as a sign of gratitude for the end of the plague epidemic that swept through Vienna until 1679. The **Column of the Plague (Pestsäule)**, by Bernhard Fischer von Erlach, includes among other images a depiction of the monarch praying, an old lady who represents the plague, the Holy Trinity and several angels. The fountains of **St. Joseph (Josefsbrunnen)** and **St. Leopold III (Leopolds-brunnen)** were built next to it in 1804.

Very close to Graben is the **Church of St. Peter (Peterskirche)**, which according to the legend was

St. Peter's Church.

KÄRNTNERSTRASSE AND KOHLMARKT.

founded by Charlemagne around 792 to commemorate his victory against the Avars. The current building dates back to the early 18th century, and stores inside it some of the best instances of Austrian Baroque.

The bustle and din of Graben extend to **Kärntnerstrasse** and **Kohlmarkt**. These three streets together with the smaller ones that criss-cross them are the pedestrian heart of downtown

SHOPPING CENTRE AT THE KÄRNTNERSTRASSE.

CAPUCHINS CHURCH.

Vienna. Here you will find the highest density of fashion shops, elegant shop-windows and charming cafés in the city. Establishments branded with the letters "K&K", standing for "*kaiserelich und königlich*" (imperial and royal), a recognition awarded by the Hapsburg to those stores that sold their products to the court, abound in this area. Kärntnerstrasse, a name that evokes the exit route toward

CAPUCHINS CHURCH: SARCOPHAGUS OF THE EMPEROR FRANZ JOSEPH.

the Austrian region of Carintia, is also popular among buskers and street artists. Some of the most outstanding buildings in this busy artery include the Casino, the Steffi shopping centre, built on the plot of land where the house where Mozart died once stood, the glass-makers Swarovski, and the so-called Austrian Workshops (Österreichische), founded by the architect Josef Hoffmann to "fill everyday life with beautiful things".

In the nearby Neuer Markt Square is the **Church of the Capuchins (Kapuzinerkirche),** an austere and modest early 17th century building that is the burial site of 12 emperors, 19 Hapsburg empresses and queens, and several noblemen. Among the monarchs buried here were Franz Joseph I and his renowned wife Sissi. The square's main monument is the **Fountain of Providence** or **Donner**, after its creator **(Donnerbrunnen).** Dating from 1739, the fountain was stripped of all of its naked figures from 1770 and 1801 under orders of Empress Maria Theresa, who considered them indecent.

Kohlmarkt, which in the past was home to the city's coal and firewood market –hence its name–, now hosts several jewellers, different design firms and "K&K" establishments. One of them is the **Demel Bakers**, deemed to be one of the best in Vienna.

The nearby Dorothhergasse Street hosts the **Hawelka Café**, a very popular venue and meeting point

NEUER MARKT (NEW MARKET) SQUARE: PROVIDENCE OR DONNER FOUNTAIN.

ALLEY THAT LEADS TO MICHAELERPLATZ. CARRIAGES ARE A COMMON MEANS TO VISIT THE CITY.

MICHAELERPLATZ ST. MICHAEL'S SQUARE AND CHURCH.

for avant-garde artists in the mid-20th century, and the **Dorotheum,** one of the world's leading auction houses.

Kohlmarkt leads to Michaelerplatz Square, the main entrance to Hofburg. But aside from boasting the façade of the Imperial Palace, the square is particularly relevant because it hosts a series of very different buildings although all of equal appeal. One of them is what was once the court's church. In-

deed, the **Church of St. Michael (Michaelerkirche)** acted as such until 1784. Despite its current appearance, the result of a large-scale restoration dating from the late 18th century, the temple was first built in the 13th century and still boasts a 14th century choir. Another outstanding building in the square is **Loos House (Looshaus).** Loyal to the principles he listed in his conference "Ornament is crime," architect

Adolf Loos designed in 1910 for the Goldmann & Salatsch tailors a very functional building that stood in sharp contrast with the kind of architecture that was most common in Vienna in those days. Dismissed as a prison and a factory by those least inclined to accept new trends, according to the legend the building was dubbed by Emperor Franz Joseph himself as "the house without eyebrows," because of its lack of cornices.

THE GRIECHENBEISL RESTAURANT. BEETHOVEN, MOZART, SCHUBERT AND WAGNER WERE AMONG ITS CLIENTS.

DOZENS OF BARS AND RESTAURANTS DOT FLEISCHMARKT AND GRIECHENGASSE STREETS. HERE, A SPOT NEXT TO GRIECHENBEISL.

One of Vienna's oldest buildings is the **Griechenbeisl ("The Greek Bite")**, an eatery located in Fleischmarkt that dates back to at least 1447. Frequented throughout history by artists and intellectuals such as Beethoven, Schubert, Wagner, Strauss and Mark Twain, this well known establishment that despite its name serves typical Viennese dishes, has witnessed significant historical events as well as all kinds of scenes of daily life. One of the anecdotes that best describes the joy for life of Vienna's dwellers is indeed set near the Griechenbeisl. One night of 1679, as the plague hit Vienna, a popular singer known as Augustine, was found unconscious on the street after having drunk himself silly in the restaurant. When he woke up, to his surprise he found he had been mistaken for dead and taken to a common grave to be incinerated. Desperate, he started playing his bagpipe and finally managed to get a passerby to help him get out. The fact that Augustine spent the night among the plague victims without falling sick himself helped bring up the spirits of the Viennese. A statue in Neustiftgasse pays tribute to this character, who is also at the origin of a folk song.

Next to the restaurant is the **Greeks' Church (Griechenkirche)**, an orthodox temple built between 1782 and 1787, just after Joseph II published his "edict on tolerance". The temple's Byzantine-styled façade, dating from 1858, is the work of architect

GREEK CHURCH.

FIGARO HOUSE.

Theophil Hansen who worked under commission from a Greek banker and ambassador named Simas.

Not far from the church is **Heiligenkreuzer Hof**, an idyllic courtyard flanked by Baroque façades whose origins can be traced to the Cistercian monastery of the Holy Cross. The oldest wall remains date back to the 12th century. An archway leads to the **"beautiful lantern alley" (Schönlatern-gasse),** so-called for the lantern that once stood here and that is now under exhibition at Wien Museum Karlsplatz. On number 7, a sandstone sculpture and a fresco depict the story of a basilisk that used to live in the well of the house of a master baker terrifying the neighbours. One day the baker placed a mirror before the beast, which died terrified of its own image.

The beautiful **Blutgasse** Street leads to **Figaro's House (Figarohaus)**, on number 5, Domgasse. This was Mozart's home from 1784 to 1787, and in it he composed "The marriage of Figaro".

DIE HOFBURG IN WIEN

Baualtersstufen
- Mittelalter
- 16. Jahrhundert
- 17. Jahrhundert
- 18. Jahrhundert
- 1. Hälfte 19. Jahrhundert
- ab 2. Hälfte 19. Jahrhundert

PALACIO IMPERIAL DE VIENA

Periodos de construcción
- Edad Media
- Siglo XVI
- Siglo XVII
- Siglo XVIII
- 1ª mitad del siglo XIX
- 2ª mitad del siglo XIX

LE PALAIS IMPERIAL DE VIENNE

Périodes de construction
- Moyen-Age
- XVIème siècle
- XVIIème siècle
- XVIIIème siècle
- 1ère moitié du XIXème siècle
- à partir de la 2ème moitié du XIXème siècle

IL PALAZZO IMPERIALE DI VIENNA

Epoche di construzione
- Medioevo
- '500
- '600
- '700
- Prima metà dell'800
- A partire dalla seconda metà dell'800

THE IMPERIAL PALACE OF VIENNA

Periods of construction
- Middle Ages
- 16th. century
- 17th. century
- 18th. century
- First half of the 19th. century
- Second half of the 19th. century

MICHAEL

SCHAUFLERGASSE

(10)

(11)

KAISER FRANZ II (I)

(12)

ELISABETH DENKMAL

THESEUSTEMPEL

VOLKSGARTEN

DR. KARL RENNER RING

ERZHG. KARL

HELDEN

BURG

BURGRING

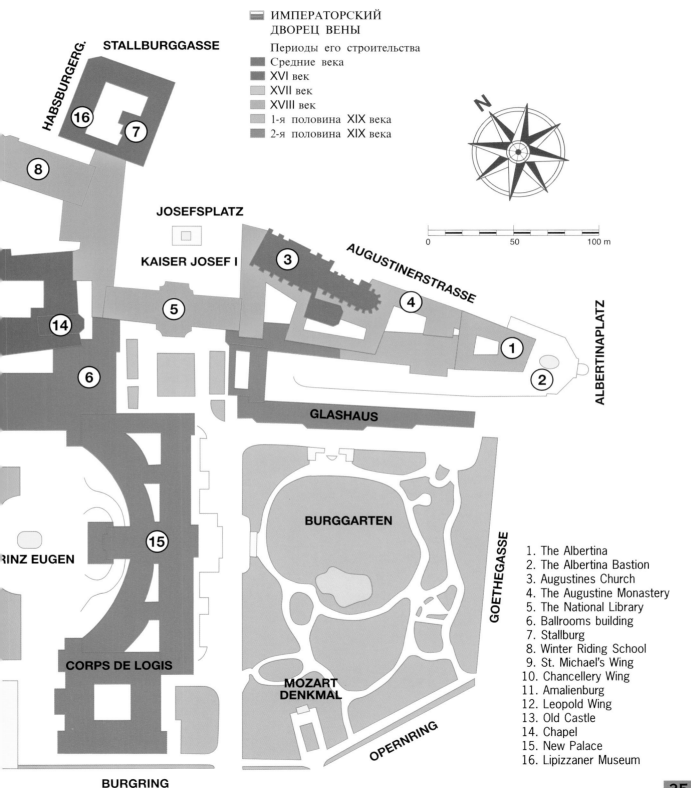

ИМПЕРАТОРСКИЙ
ДВОРЕЦ ВЕНЫ

Периоды его строительства

Средние века
XVI век
XVII век
XVIII век
1-я половина XIX века
2-я половина XIX века

STALLBURGGASSE

HABSBURGERG.

JOSEFSPLATZ

KAISER JOSEF I

AUGUSTINERSTRASSE

ALBERTINAPLATZ

GLASHAUS

BURGGARTEN

GOETHEGASSE

RINZ EUGEN

CORPS DE LOGIS

MOZART DENKMAL

OPERNRING

BURGRING

1. The Albertina
2. The Albertina Bastion
3. Augustines Church
4. The Augustine Monastery
5. The National Library
6. Ballrooms building
7. Stallburg
8. Winter Riding School
9. St. Michael's Wing
10. Chancellery Wing
11. Amalienburg
12. Leopold Wing
13. Old Castle
14. Chapel
15. New Palace
16. Lipizzaner Museum

SWISS DOOR.

comprises 18 semi-independent buildings, 19 courtyards, 54 different staircases and 2,600 rooms, is extraordinarily beautiful. The unique structure of the building can be explained by the habit among Austrian monarchs to never occupy the rooms of their immediate predecessors, as such embarking on constant new building projects.

The Imperial Palace (Hofburg) was constructed upon a 13th century castle. All that remains of the latter is the Gothic apse of the palace's **chapel (Burgkapelle).** In it every Sunday the renowned Vienna's Boys' Choir performs in mass. Founded in 1498, this internationally renowned choir has had among its members Franz Schubert and Josef Haydn. The chapel is located in the **Courtyard of the Swiss (Schweizerhof),** the oldest part of the ancient castle. The courtyard can be reached via the **Swiss Gate (Schweizertor),** built in the mid-16th century in Renaissance style under orders of Emperor Ferdinand I. The courtyard is also linked to the late 16th century **Amalia Palace (Amelienburg),** the home of Empress Elizabeth, best known as Sissi. Among the different rooms occupied by this historic figure whose life has been brought to the screen several times, particularly interesting is a small gym, her bedroom and the exhibition that traces her tragic death in Geneva at the hands of an anarchist in 1898. Also in the courtyard, the **Treasury Chamber (Schatzkammer)** gathers pieces of great value, which range from the jewels of Empress Maria Theresa and the symbols and insignia carried by the Hapsburg during

What was for 700 years the residence of the Hapsburg Dynasty –to be more precise from the 13th century to 1918, when the Republic was proclaimed– is in fact a cluster of buildings erected at different times and as such in different styles that present no homogeneity, nor do they try to do so. Despite this, this heterogeneous compound, which

PORTRAITS OF EMPEROR FRANZ JOSEPH I AND HIS WIFE ELIZABETH.

HABSBURG MONARCHS OF AUSTRIA

Rudolf I (1218-1291), 1276-1282
Albert I (ca. 1250-1308),1282-1298
Rudolf III (1281-1307), 1298-1306
Frederick I the Fair (1286-1330),1306-1330
Albert V (II) (1397-1439) (1404) 1411-1439
Frederick V (III) (1415-1493), 1439-1490

Maximilian I (1459-1519), 1490-1519
Charles V (1500-1558),1519-1521
Ferdinand I (1503-1564), 1521-1564
Maximilian II (1527-1576), 1564-1576
Rudolf II (1552-1612)
Matthias (1557-1619)

Ferdinand II (1578-1637), 1619-1637
Ferdinand III (1608-1657), 1637-1657
Leopold I (1640-1705),1657-1705
Josef I (1678-1711), 1705-1711
Charles VI (1685-1740), 1711-1740
Maria Theresa (1717-1780),1740-1780

Josef II (1741-1790), 1765-1790
Leopold II (1747-1792), 1790-1792
Franz II (1768-1835), 1792-1835
Ferdinand I (1793-1875), 1835-1848
Franz Josef I (1830-1916), 1848-1916
Charles I (1887-1922) 1916-1918

TREASURY CHAMBER: HAPSBURG CROWN, IMPERIAL GLOBE AND STAFF.

crowning ceremonies to the christening dress of Franz Joseph I and a bone that according to the legend belonged to St. Anne.

It is also possible to visit the **Emperor's Apartment (Kaiser Appartements),** located in the **Chancellory wing (Reichskanzleitrakt),** dating from the 18th century. Transformed into a museum, the emperor's dwellings include the hall where the court's acts were held, the conference room in which Emperor Franz

PALACE DINING ROOM.

CHANCELLERY WING:
FRANZ JOSEPH I'S MEETING ROOM AND
BEDROOM.

Joseph met with his cabinet and the emperor's room and bathroom. Great exponents of the splendour of imperial Austria, almost all the rooms are exuberantly and sumptuously decorated, with numerous stuccoes, tapestries, Bohemian glass lamps, china, porcelain heaters and Louis XV furniture. More austere is Franz Joseph I's room. This emperor's statue stands in the courtyard outside the imperial apartments.

BURGPLATZ: MONUMENT TO EMPEROR FRANZ I AND IN THE BACKGROUND THE AMALIA PALACE.

LEOPOLDINE
WING:
RESIDENCE
OF THE HEAD
OF STATE.

Dating from the 16th century, the **royal stables (Stallburg)** were also built by Emperor Ferdinand I, but the building's aim was different than what its name indicates. The majestic structure was meant to become the residence of the emperor's son Maximilian II, but he never moved in and was eventually transformed to host the royal stables. Today, aside from housing the horses of the Spanish Riding School, the building also houses an art gallery.

In the 17th century, Emperor Leopold commissioned from his favourite architect, Fischer von Erlach, a restructuring project devised to unite the different buildings that made up the compound. The result is the **Leopoldine Wing (Leopoldtrakt),** currently the residence of the President of the Republic.

From the 18th century are the imperial Library, now the **National Library (Nationalbibliothek),** the **winter manège (Winterreitschule)**, where the performances by the Spanish Riding School now take place, and the **ballrooms' wing (Redoutensaaltrakt).**

Construction did not slow down in the 19th century, rather the opposite is true. It was in this century when the project for the astounding façade on Michaelerplatz , the Hofburg's **main entrance**, was designed. Topped by a green dome, the neo-Baroque façade includes large statues depicting scenes from Hercules' life, as well as two lateral fountains with allegorical figures referring to "the power of the sea" and "the power of the

JOSEFSPLATZ (JOSEPH SQUARE): EQUESTRIAN STATUE OF EMPEROR JOSEPH II AND NATIONAL LIBRARY.

MICHAELERPLATZ:
MAIN ENTRY TO
THE HOFBURG.

HEROES' SQUARE: MONUMENT TO PRINCE EUGENE OF SAVOY.

earth". No less awe-inspiring is the area known as **New Palace (Neue Burg).** Built between 1881 and 1914, it represents the compound's last great expansion. The semicircular building embraces **Heldenplatz** or **Heroes' Square**, where stand the statutes of Prince Eugene of Savoy and of Archduke Charles. The building hosts several sections of the National Library, and different arms and musical instruments collections, as well as the Ephesus Museum.

THE SPANISH RIDING SCHOOL

One of the most interesting buildings in the Imperial Palace is the one hosting the Spanish Riding School (Spanische Reitschule), so named because in its early days its horses came from Spain. The Baroque structure dates from 1728 to 1735 and was built by Fischer von Erlach to house an institution that is unique in the world and that has preserved virtually unchanged the classical riding style. Wearing their

THE FAÇADE OF THE SPANISH RIDING SCHOOL, IN JOSEFSPLATZ.

SPANISH RIDING SCHOOL.
© SPANISCHE HOFREITSCHULE.

double horned hats and brown tailcoats, the riders can make their lipizzan horses –"the emperor's white horses"– perform precise and elegant moves to the rhythm of the music in a room with 46 columns, stuccoed walls and ceiling, and huge glass lamps. Some 10 years of training are required to become an expert rider. The show is without a doubt one of Vienna's most fascinating attractions, both for its beauty as for the wonderful facility where it takes place.

LIPIZZAN MUSEUM

The old pharmacy of the Imperial Palace now hosts the Lipizzan Museum, which traces the history of the famous white horses with Spanish-Arab blood that, brought over from Spain, where reared from 1580 to 1918 in the then Austrian town of Lip- izza, which is now in Slovenia. The exhibition includes paintings on equestrian subjects, uniforms and different riding objects. One of the highlights is the carriage of Crown Prince Rudolf, the son of Empress Sissi and Emperor Franz Joseph. A sound-proof and

NATIONAL LIBRARY: MAIN FAÇADE AND HOMAGE HALL.

a reflecting window allows visitors to look into the Riding School's stables.

NATIONAL LIBRARY

Considered one of the most beautiful libraries in the world, the National Library (Nationalbibliothek) is housed in one of the wings of the Imperial Palace, across from Josefsplatz Square. It was built by Fischer von Erlach in the early 18th century in Baroque style. The main hall is the most spectacular. It is almost 80 meters long and 20 meters tall and is crowned by a dome decorated with frescoes by Daniel Gran. At the centre of the hall stands a statue of Charles VI. Among its important collection, made up by over two and a half million books, are 15,000 volumes drawn from Prince Eugene of Savoy's library, and a wide-ranging collection of documents on Luther's Reformation. Also run by the National Library is the interesting Globe Museum, the Music Hall, exhibiting original scores by Haydn, Mozart and Strauss, and the Esperanto Museum.

AUGUSTINES CHURCH

Although its rococo decoration might mislead visitors into thinking otherwise, the Augustines Church (Augustinerkirche) is a 14th century Gothic temple built on the western end of the Imperial Palace. As the official church of the Viennese court, it hosted im-

ALBERTINAPLATZ: AUGUSTINES CHURCH.

portant religious events including the weddings of Empress Maria Theresa and Franz Stephan von Lothringen in 1736; Franz Joseph and Sissi's in 1854; Crown Prince Rudolf and Princess Stephanie's in 1881; and even that of French Emperor Napoleon with Marie Louise, in 1810. At the same time it hosts the hearts of 54 Austrian emperors and monarchs, placed in urns on display that the Loretto Chapel. The beauty of the sepulchre of Princess Marie Christine, a classic-styled work in Carrara marble built by the Italian artist Antonio Canova from 1798 to 1805 and that depicts through its figures the sadness and pain caused by the death of a loved one, is awe-inspiring.

The building also witnessed the first ever rendition of Franz Schubert's Mass in F major and Anton Bruckner's Mass in F minor, and its masses on Sundays and religious holidays are still extremely popular.

THE ALBERTINA
This sumptuous dwelling located on the southern tip of the Imperial Palace is named after a collection of prints and drawings begun in 1776 by Albert of Saxony, the son-in-law of Empress Maria Theresa. The most important of its kind in the world,

LIT UP SIGNS AT THE ALBERTINA, WHICH HAS ONE OF THE WORLD'S LARGEST PRINT COLLECTIONS.

ALBERTINAPLATZ: MONUMENT TO ARCHDUKE ALBERT AND THE DANUBE FOUNTAIN.

the Albertina collection brings together some one million prints and 60,000 drawings. Among its most outstanding pieces are Durer's "Hare," Gustav Klimt's sketches for his "Beethoven Frieze" and the portraits and nudes by Egon Schiele. Aside from its permanent exhibition, this residential palace is the largest in the Hofburg, and also hosts temporary exhibitions that display works by Rubens, Cézanne and Picasso. One of the most recent exhibitions hosted here was devoted to architecture and photography and put on display works by artists such as Helmut Newton and Lisette Model among others.

Outside, on the **Albertinaplatz** stands the interesting 1869 Danube Fountain, restored in 1989. On the same square is a 1998 sculpture in tribute to the victims of Fascism.

ALBERTINA-PLATZ: 1998 SCULPTURE IN TRIBUTE TO THE VICTIMS OF FASCISM.

URANIA CULTURAL SOCIETY AND GOVERNMENT BUILDING.

On December 20, 1857 Emperor Franz Joseph I signed a decree that would change for good the appearance of old Vienna. The time had come to tear down the medieval walls that hindered the city's growth and to design a large avenue that would symbolise at once the greatness of imperial Austria and the power of its young but flourishing bourgeoisie. The project included the construction of majestic buildings surrounded by gardens and several monuments and statues. All sectors of society and the economy were to be represented in this ambitious project that was partly inspired by the Parisian boulevards. The first stage was completed in 1865, when on May 1 the emperor inaugurated the first part of the Ring (Ringstrasse), Vienna's most sumptuous avenue. Most of its classic-styled buildings had been erected by 1880, although the building works continued until the early 20th century.

Stretching over four kilometres and almost 60-meters-wide, the Ring surrounds Vienna's old town, the so-called inner city (Innere Stadt). The avenue, which in Franz Joseph's words was meant to "beautify my imperial and residential capital," hosts some of the most representative public buildings of the capital, as well as significant private compounds, squares and parks, hotels and several distinguished cafés.

Walking clockwise, the first interesting pit stop is the **Urania Cultural Society.** This 1910 building by the *Jugendstil* architect Max Fabiani, a follower of Otto Wagner, is the headquarters of an astronomical society and includes an observatory as well as several screening and conference rooms. Next to it is the **Government's Building (Regierungsgebäude),** which was at first the Austrian government's War Ministry. Built in neo-Baroque style between 1909 and 1913, on its roof it boasts a large two-headed eagle with a 16-metre wingspan. Across from this building, which currently houses several ministries, is the **Post Savings Bank (Postsparkasse),** one of the best exponents of *Jugendstil* architecture. Its author, Otto Wagner, was one of the most prominent representatives of the movement that came to be known as "secession" (Sezession), which called for a new kind of art to counter the historicism that ruled at the time. Dating from 1906 and char-

POST SAVINGS BANK.

APPLIED ARTS MUSEUM.

acterised by its simplicity, the building is known by Vienna's dwellers as "the house of the rivets," for the abundance of the latter on its façade. In the nearby **Applied Arts Museum (Museum für angewandte Kunst-MAK)**, built from 1868 to 1877 by Heinrich von Ferstel, it is possible to admire several objects, including furniture, jewels, ceramics and even leather articles, made during the apogee of the *Jugendstil* period.

A landscape painter, Josef Selleny, and the municipal gardener

CITY PARK AND THE KURSALON.

Rudolf Siebeck, were charged with designing the beautiful **City Park (Stadtpark)**, officially inaugurated in 1862. Following the English style, the park is one of the favoured outdoor spots among the Viennese. It has a concert pavilion, the Kursalon, a large lake and statues representing some of Austria's leading composers, including Johann Strauss', which is perhaps one of the most photographed monuments in Vienna. Aside from the golden figure of the king of waltz, dating from 1921, it is also possible to see the statues of Schubert, Lehar, Bruckner and Stolz.

The first of the Ring's buildings to be completed was **The State Opera House (Staatsoper)**. It opened its doors in 1869 and the first opera performed in it was Mozart's "Don Giovanni". The architects in charge of the project,

CITY PARK: MONUMENTS TO JOHANN STRAUSS AND SCHUBERT.

STATE OPERA HOUSE.

August Sicard von Sicardsburg and Eduard van der Nüll, were harshly criticised for their work. Apparently even Emperor Franz Joseph expressed some reservations over the final result. People did not like the Opera House and they expressed their distaste calling it the "sunken box". The pressure was such that Van der Nüll, who was in charge of the building's interior design, committed suicide hanging himself, and von Sicardsburg, responsible for the structure as a whole, died from a

THE OPERA'S CONCERT HALL.

STATE OPERA HOUSE: FIRST FLOOR.

heart attack two months after his colleague had passed away.

Despite the old controversy, this Renaissance-styled building is one of the most impressive of the Ring. A few days before the end of World War Second, it was almost completely destroyed by bombs. The only elements left standing were the box, the hallway, the main stairway and a tearoom. It was rebuilt strictly following the original project, but its facilities were updated. It was re-inaugurated in 1955 with Beethoven's "Fidelio", which was also broadcast on television.

The quality of its orchestra, strengthened by members of the Vienna Philharmonic, the standing of its conductors –including Gustav Mahler, Richard Strauss, Herbert von Karajan and Karl Böhm–, and the demanding audience that fills the 2,200 seats in the hall, have made this one of the best opera houses in the world.

Behind the Opera House is the **Sacher Hotel**, famous because of its founder, the baker who

SACHER HOTEL.

BURGGARTEN (PALACE GARDENS): THE PALMENHAUS GREENHOUSE.

created the internationally renowned Sachertorte. Indeed, Franz Sacher was the first one to make, in 1832, this delicious sponge cake with melted chocolate and jam that has become, for its quality and taste, one of Vienna's symbols.

A bit further down the Ring is the **Burggarten** Park. Built in 1819, this beautiful garden houses the old and beautiful greenhouse of the Imperial Palace, the Palmenhaus, which is currently a café and restaurant. Also interesting are the Butterfly House (Schemetterlinghaus) and Mozart's statue, dating from 1896.

Standing across from each other, the **Natural History Museum (Naturhistorisches Museum)** and **the Art History Museum (Kunsthistorisches Museum-KHM)** are two almost identical Renaissance buildings, built between 1872 and 1881 by architects Gottfried Semper and Karl von Hasenauer. The former hosts interesting exhibitions in the fields of geology, palaeontology, prehistory, botanic, zoology and mineralogy. The mineralogy collection is considered the oldest of its kind in Europe. On the other hand, the Art History Museum, holds the wide-ranging collec-

tions of the Hapsburg, whose origins date as far back as the late 13th century. Its painting gallery, one of the most outstanding in the world, holds works by Rubens, Rembrandt, Brueghel, Durer, Titian, Raphael and Velázquez. Also, the Museum includes sections devoted to Ancient Egypt, exhibiting original columns from Luxor, the Antiquity, the Middle Ages and the Modern Age. Among the pieces on show is Benvenuto Cellini's famous golden salt shaker, a small but notable example of Baroque art.

The two museums flank Maria-Theresien Platz, where it is pos-

MONUMENT TO
MOZART
(BURGGARTEN).

NATURAL
HISTORY
MUSEUM.

ART HISTORY
MUSEUM.

ART HISTORY MUSEUM: "DIANA AND CALLISTO," BY TITIAN; "HELENA FOURMENT," BY PIETER PAUL RUBENS, AND "MADONNA WITH ST. JOHN AND THE CHILD," ALSO KNOWN AS "THE MADONNA OF THE MEADOW," BY RAPHAEL.

"WEDDING BANQUET,"
BY PIETER BRUEGHEL
(ART HISTORY MUSEUM).

sible to visit the **monument to Empress Maria-Theresa (Denkmal der Kaiserin Maria Theresia).** Sculpted in 1887 by Kaspar von Zumbusch and Karl Hasenauer, it shows the empress surrounded by her generals mounting horses and her councillors. It is also possible to see a bas-relief depicting Mozart as a child, as well as others depicting Haydn

MONUMENT TO EMPRESS MARIA THERESA.

VOLKSGARTEN GARDENS: THESEUS TEMPLE. IN THE BACKGROUND THE CITY HALL TOWER AND THE NATIONAL THEATRE.

and Gluck. There are also several allegories of strength, intelligence, justice and benevolence.

On the other side of the Ringstrasse, after passing the last Hofburg buildings, is the **People's Garden (Volksgarten),** inaugurated in 1823. It was erected on the spot where the rampart of the Imperial Palace blown up by the French in 1809 once stood. In the middle of these pleasant surroundings there are two particularly interesting works. First the Theseus Temple, inspired by the Teseion of Athens, and the other the monument in tribute of Empress Sissi, built in 1907.

Ancient Greece also served as inspiration for Theophil von Hansen, the architect who designed the **Parliament (Parlament).** The choice of this distant historical reference was not irrelevant. Considering it was meant to be the house of democracy, von Hansen chose to pay this small, personal tribute to the birthplace of parliamentary life. Built between 1873 and 1883, the building oozes classicism. Over

VOLKSGARTEN GARDEN: MONUMENT TO EMPRESS ELIZABETH.

30 sculptors participated in the works and materials from every single one of the nations that formed the empire were used in its construction, to symbolise "the confluence of all the forces of the kingdoms and countries represented in the Imperial Council (Reichsrat)". In 1902 Carl Kundmann erected the Palas Atenea Fountain across from the Parliament's main façade. Next to the goddess of wisdom is the winged goddess of victory, Nike, as well as two other figures, one holding up the tablets of the law, as a tribute to the legislative tasks of Parliament, and the other holding up a sword, a symbol of the administration and justice.

Next to the Parliament is the **City Hall (Rathaus),** the most important neo-Gothic civic building in Vienna. Designed by the German architect Friedrich von Schmidt, who had previously directed the building works at Cologne Cathedral, it was erected from 1872 to 1883.

Its central tower, almost 100-meters-tall, is crowned by a copper statue of a soldier that is 3.4 meters tall and weighs 1.8 tonnes. The so-called "City Hall man" (Rathausmann) was hoisted to those heights through a complicated process using reels of cable and steam engines. Almost one century later the "City Hall man" was brought down to be restored and then placed back on top of the tower again, but this time by a helicopter.

PARLIAMENT AND THE SCULPTURE OF PALLAS ATHENE.

THE CITY HALL. EVERY SUMMER EVENING CULTURAL EVENTS TAKE PLACE IN ITS GARDENS.

Two fountains, several statues, including those of two legendary waltz composers —Johan Strauss senior and Joseph Lanner—, plants and exotic trees, and a large lime tree planted to commemorate the 50th anniversary of Franz Joseph I's government, are some of the elements filling up the Rathausplatz or City Hall Square. This popular spot, transformed into an ice skating rink every New Year's Eve, also has a beautiful park designed in 1873 by Rudolf Siebeck, who also designed the City Park. It is also the stage for different cultural and social events organized by the City Council throughout the year. Without a doubt, the most charming of the events that take place here is the Christkindlmarkt or Christmas market, which first took place some 700 years ago. From mid-November to Christmas Eve, children and adults cluster around the close to 150 stands, allowing themselves to be transported into a magical world by their wide range of wares, including toys, carousels, sweets, nativity scenes and Christmas decorations. Every year some three million people are estimated to visit the Rathausplatz market to relish in the Christmas spirit. There are other Christmas bazaars in Vienna, such as that of Schönbrunn Palace, that of Freyung Street and the Am Hof market, but none of them have such a long history or are as popular as the Chirstkindlmarkt.

Across from the City Hall rises the imposing silhouette of the **National Theatre (Burgtheater)**, the oldest of Vienna's theatres and the first monumental building lit up by electric power. The building works stretched from 1874 to 1888, following a project by Gottfried Semper and Karl Hasenauer inspired by Italian Renaissance art. Despite some acoustic problems

UNIVERSITY AND MONUMENT IN TRIBUTE OF LIEBENBERG.

early on that were soon solved, the theatre's inauguration was much vaunted across Europe and it soon became the continent's leading German-speaking theatre. Rebuilt in 1955 to repair damage resulting from World War Second, the theatre's façade is decorated by the busts of legendary poets such as Shakespeare, Calderón, Molière, Goethe and Schiller, while the inside boasts two large staircases and two lavishly decorated halls. The **University (Universität)** building, offers another unavoidable encounter with the city's intellectual and cultural spirit. Founded by Rudolf IV in 1365, it was built, like the National Theatre, according to the parameters of Italian Renaissance art by architect Heinrich von Festel. The latter died of tuberculosis one year before the building's official inauguration in 1884. Particularly interesting are the cloister, with the Castalia Fountain at its centre, the Aula Magna and the Library. On the façade of what is considered the oldest university in German-speaking coun-

THE DREIMÄDERLHAUS, AT THE MELK BASTION.

PASQUALATI HOUSE.

tries stands out a depiction of Pallas Athene's birth.

Across from the University stands the monument to one of the most popular mayor's in the city's history, Johann Andreas von Liebenberg, who played a key role in the defence of Vienna during the Turkish siege of 1683 and the **Melk Bastion (Mölker Bastei)**, one of the oldest parts of the city. Also here is **Pasqualati House,** which has gone down in history for being Beethoven's house from 1804 to 1808. In it the composer created works such as the opera *Fidelio*. On February 13, 1853, a Hungarian separatist unsuccessfully tried to kill Franz Joseph I by stabbing him twice on the neck. His brother, Archduke Maximilian, who years later would become Emperor of Mexico, decided to build

VOTIVE CHURCH.

a church on the spot where the failed attack had taken place. This is the reason behind the construction of the **Votive Church (Votivkirche)**. The building works stretched from 1855 to 1879, when it was consecrated coinciding with the celebration of the emperor's and Sissi's silver wedding. The idea was for the church to become a mausoleum for celebrated Austrians. In practice, however, only Niklas Slam, who defended the city from the 1529 Turkish at-

tack, was buried there. Heinrich von Ferstel, the architect responsible for the Votive Church, found inspiration for his project in French cathedrals. The building is considered one of the best exponents of Vienna's neo-Gothic style. Two, almost 100-meter-tall towers flank the entrance. Inside stands out the Antwerp altar, from the 15th century, bought by Franz Joseph I for his private collection. Also noteworthy is the Guadeloupe Madonna altar, created in tribute to the

Emperor of Mexico, Maximilian, who died in the Latin American country in 1867.

The last great building in the Ringstrasse, already in the heart of the Scots Ring, is the **Stock Exchange (Börse)**, by Theophil von Hansen. Of Renaissance style, it was built between 1874 and 1877 in a plot of land donated by Franz Joseph I. In 1956 a devastating fire completely destroyed the brokers' hall, which only became fully operational again in 1959.

THE STOCK EXCHANGE.

SCHWARZENBERG CAFÉ.

SCHWARZENBERGPLATZ: MONUMENT TO THE RED ARMY.

Two palaces, that of Archduke Louis Victor and the Wertheim Palace, flank this 19th century square designed to frame the equestrian statue of Karl Fürst zu Schwarzenberg, an Austrian soldier who attained glory in the battlefield but also in the sphere of diplomacy, as he was the one to set up Napoleon's wedding with Marie Louise of Austria. On one of the edges of the square the authorities of the defunct Soviet Union erected a monument in tribute of Red Army soldiers who died during the liberation of Vienna in World War Second.

The building works on the palace of Archduke Louis Victor, currently used for the rehearsals of the Burgtheater, started in 1864 under orders of Franz Joseph I. The name of the lavish mansion indicates what its final object was meant to be, but the fact is that Louis Victor, the emperor's youngest brother, never inhabited it. The Wertheim Palace, on the other hand, was the residence of this Austrian businessman and inventor of anti-fire safes. At the mansion's inauguration ball, in 1869, Joseph Strauss presented for the first time his French polka Feuerfestpolka. Two other significant buildings help highlight the beauty of this square. They are the Schwarzenberg Palace, which is now a hotel, and the French Embassy.

HOUSE OF THE FRIENDS OF MUSIC.

Karlsplatz or St. Charles Square, with its buildings, terraces and gardens, is one of Vienna's great public spaces and also a relevant urban communications hub. Onto it face buildings as legendary as the **House of the friends of Music (Musikverein),** an institution founded in 1814 that has a library, an archive and several collections including one of musical instruments and another

HOUSE OF THE FRIENDS OF MUSIC: GOLDEN ROOM.

TECHNICAL UNIVERSITY.

of scores, as well as two concert halls. The main hall, known as Golden Hall, can host 2,000 viewers and 500 musicians and is the traditional venue of the New Year's Eve concert, broadcast around the world. Designed by Teophil Hansen in 1870, the building is also the headquarters of the celebrated Vienna Philharmonic.

Next to the Musikverein is the **Artists House (Künstlerhaus)**, once the headquarters of the Austrian Association of Plastic Artists. Built in 1868, it currently hosts architecture and design exhibitions and also doubles up as a space for experimental theatre and cinema.

On one end of Karlsplatz stands the classicist building of the **Technical University (Technische Universität),** and on the other the **Wien Museum Karlsplatz**, which traces the city's history from its origins to the present.

In the square's main park stand several statutes, including one of composer Johannes Brahms, who died nearby, and of the inventors Josef Ressel, who invented ship propellers, Josef Madersperger, who invented the sewing machine and Siegfried Marcus, who invented the internal combustion engine.

In the heart of Karlsplatz it is possible to admire one of the greatest exponents of *Jugendstil* architecture: one of the **pavilions** for the subway station designed by **Otto Wagner** in 1899. Familiar with the principles of this artistic movement that countered the official architecture so well-represented in the Ringstrasse, Wagner set up these prefabricated steel structures with in-

MUNICIPAL MUSEUM.

dustrially produced abundant floral decorations.

But the square's true landmark is the **St. Charles Borromeo Church (Karlskirche),** which many consider to be Vienna's most beautiful Baroque temple. Its history is tied to the promise made by Charles VI in 1713 to celebrate the end of plague epidemic that had swept through the city. The emperor was certainly aware of the important role the saint, then Bishop of Milano, played during

OTTO WAGNER PAVILION.

ST. CHARLES
BORROMEO
CHURCH.

ST. CHARLES BORROMEO: DETAIL OF THE HIGH ALTAR AND OF THE PAINTINGS OF MASTER J. M. ROTTMAYR, PRESENT ACROSS THE INTERIOR OF THE CHURCH.

the plague that swept through the Lombard capital between 1576 and 1578. He commissioned the project to Johann Bernhard Fischer von Erlach, the great Baroque architect of the time, who set in motion the project in 1716. The architect died as the project was still under construction and it was his son, Joseph Emanuel, who had to complete it in 1739.

Oval-shaped, the temple consists of a great central nave topped by a 72-meter-high dome on which the artist Johannes Michael Rottmayr painted the scene of the saint's glorification. Its façade, with a six-column portico and two statues on either side is reminiscent of Greek temples. The church is flanked by two 33 meter tall columns decorated with scenes from the life of St. Charles and topped by the crowns and imperial eagles of the Hapsburg dynasty.

HENRY MOORE SCULPTURE, IN ST. CHARLES SQUARE.

In 1897, 19 proponents of a more democratic kind of art less tied to the academic and economic guidelines of the times decided to break away from the Artists House to create their own association. This new institution, backed by creators such as Gustav Klimt, Joseph Hoffmann, Joseph Maria Olbrich and the architect Otto Wagner, had an exhibition hall that would display the essence of their proposals. Thus, and thanks to the financing of the industrial magnate Karl Wittgenstein, the father of the philosopher Ludwig Wittgenstein and the donation of the plot by the City Hall, in 1898 Olbrich designed a cube-like pavilion that came to be known as the Secession Palace (Sezession). The building is topped by a dome decorated by 3,000 golden iron laurel leaves. On the façade it is possible to see three masks that symbolise painting, architecture and sculpture and the motto "Ver Sacrum" (Sacred Spring). Inside, one of the highlights is Gustav Klimt's 34-meter-long frieze inspired by Beethoven's Ninth Symphony. The Secession movement called for a new aesthetic based on the predominance of floral elements and curved shapes, as well as the abolition of the differences between Fine and Applied Arts. This innovative concept of art was taking root across different European countries, each developing their own national peculiarities within it. In Great Britain, where it started thriving in the 1880s, it was dubbed Modern Style, in Spain it came to be known as Modernismo, in France as Art Nouveau, in Italy as Liberty or Stile Floreale and in Germany as Jugendstil, or youth style.

SEZESSION BUILDING.

NASCHMARKT.

FLOHMARKT.

variety of ingredients and spices, from the most rare and sophisticated products imported from remote areas of the world to the most common products found in Austrian kitchens. On Saturday, **Flohmarkt**, the second-hand and bargains market, adds to the usual bustle of the Naschmarkt. These kinds of flea-markets are extremely popular in Vienna and as such several Flohmarkt take place across the Austrian capital.

Somewhat hidden from the markets' usual din stands the **An Der Wien Theatre.** This institution opened its doors in 1801 and had soon attained great prestige. Directed by Mozart's librettist Emanuel Schikaneder, it was the stage for the premières of works such as Beethoven's "Fidelio". Today it hosts some of the leading international musicals.

Established in 1774 and functioning as we know it today since 1819, the **Naschmarkt** is a food market that is open Monday to Satur- day. In it, it is possible to buy food products, have a snack and taste more elaborate recipes. The stalls, brimming with colours, flavours and smells, offer a great

AN DER WIEN THEATRE.

DETAIL OF THE MAJOLIKAHAUS, BY OTTO WAGNER, AT 40, LINKE WIENZEILE.

HOUSE BY OTTO WAGNER, DECORATED WITH GOLDEN MEDALLIONS BY KOLO MOSER, AT 38, LINKE WIENZEILE (ACROSS FROM THE NASCHMARKT).

Stretching across 60,000 square meters, Vienna's **MuseumsQuartier (MQ)** is among the world's 10 largest cultural areas. Its facilities, including over 40 buildings, do not just house museums, exhibition halls and other artistic projects, but also court-yards, gardens, terraces, restaurants and stores, creating value added to its already appealing cultural offer. Although this so-called Museums Quarter was only officially inaugurated as such in 2001, its origins date back to 1723, the year the architects Fischer von Erlach –father and son– completed the stables commissioned by Charles VI. The building has the longest Baroque façade in Vienna –350-meters-long– and was extended in 1853 with the construction of an indoor manège under commission of Franz Joseph I. In 1921 the building started hosting exhibitions and trade shows and by the 1980s the project to create an entire neighbourhood devoted to culture started taking shape.

From an architectonic perspective the most striking elements of the MuseumsQuartier are its most recent buildings. Cube-shaped, they are buried 15 meters into the ground. The lighter cube is the Leopold Museum, which hosts the largest collection of modern Austrian art, including works of Egon Schiele. The darker cube is the head-quarters of the Mumok (the Modern Art Museum of Vienna's Ludwig Foundation), which focuses on contemporary art. The Kunsthalle Wien hall has specialized in international contemporary art while the Architekurzentrum organises thematic exhibitions aiming to bolster the debate over contemporary architecture. At the MuseumsQuartier there is also a museum for the youngest members of the family, the ZoomKindermuseum.

Founded in 1889 under the initiative of a group of Viennese dwellers who wanted an alternative to the Ringstrasse's National Theater, the **People's Theatre (Volkstheater)** is a historicist building that had as

MUSEUMSQUARTIER (MQ).

78

PEOPLE'S THEATRE.

its goal from the start to bring the classics to the general public. As such, the institution's managers adopted a policy of affordable prices for all in exchange, however, for increasing the number of seats to limits that would now be deemed unacceptable. Later reforms reduced its capacity but increased comfort and the visibility. With almost 1,000 seats, the People's Theatre is still today one of the largest theatres in German-speaking countries.

THE PALAIS TRAUTSON (HEADQUARTERS OF THE JUSTICE MINISTRY), VERY CLOSE TO THE PEOPLE'S THEATRE.

ocated on a soft hill overlooking Vienna's old quarter, the Belvedere palaces were built between 1700 and 1725 upon a project by architect Johann Lucas von Hildebrandt. They were meant to become the summer residence of Prince Eugene of Savoy, but in practice only the lower palace (Unteres Belvedere), the first one to be built, was used as a summer retreat by the great hero of the war against the Turks. The upper palace (Oberes Belvedere) was used to host official receptions and parties aimed at enhancing the prince's popularity. A fantastic garden in three levels designed by Dominique Girard separates these two wonderful Baroque buildings.

A few years after the prince's death the estate was acquired by Em-

ENTRANCE TO THE BELVEDERE.

press Maria Theresa in 1752. Some time later, following an idea of her husband Joseph II, the two palaces were used to show to the public for the first time the imperial painting collections.

On May 15, 1955, the Marble Hall of the upper Belvedere was used to sign the International Austrian Treaty by which the country regained its independence after the Allied occupation after World War Second. In 1997 the Belvedere was transformed into one of Vienna's leading museums. The lower palace houses the Austrian Baroque Museum, displaying a collection of 17th and 18th century paintings and sculptures, and the Austrian Museum of Medieval Art. The upper palace, on the other hand, traces the past 1,000 years of Austrian art and includes a 19th and 20th century art gallery that displays several legendary works including Gustav Klimt's "The Kiss" and others by artists such as Schiele and Kokoschka.

LOWER BELVEDERE AND GARDENS.

UPPER BELVEDERE PALACE.

UPPER BELVEDERE: ENTRANCE AND GREAT MARBLE HALL.

HUNDERTWASSE HOUSE.

The **Hundertwasser House** is a council building named after its author, the controversial Viennese painter Friedensreich Hundertwasser (1928-2000). The artist who criticised excessive rationalism in architecture designed a colourful building without right angles and straight walls. It was built from 1983 to 1985, and financed

KUNSTHAUS WIEN.

by a City Council that was at the time very close to environmentalist positions. Despite the controversy it sparked, Hundertwasser House has become a true tourist attraction. The work and ideology of this unique artist can be explored through his paintings, architecture models and drawings exhibited at the **Kunsthaus Wien** museum, which also organises temporary exhibitions focusing on the work of other artists.

THERMOELECTRIC POWER STATION REDESIGNED BY HUNDERTWASSER NEXT TO THE DANUBE CANAL.

THE PRATER AND ITS FUN PARK
AS SEEN FROM THE TOP OF
THE WHEEL.

It was emperor Josef II who in 1766 decided to give to the Viennese people as a gift this old hunting reserve that until then could only be accessed by the imperial family and the nobility. From that point on the Prater started drawing hundreds of visitors and street artists and food stalls and taverns sprung up with them. On occasion of the 1873 Universal Exhibition, this 1,300-hectare expanse of greenery

DIFFERENT RIDES AT THE PRATER.

consolidated itself as a major recreational spot. Some years later, in 1897, to celebrate the 50th anniversary of the crowning of Emperor Franz Joseph I, the British engineer Walter Basset designed a huge wheel (Riesenrad) that is 65 meters tall and weighs 430 tonnes. With time, especially after it was featured in Carol Reed's feature "The Third Man", it became one of Vienna's landmarks. The panoramic view from the top of the wheel is without a doubt an unforgettable experience.

At the Prater you will find over 250 rides for all ages, outdoor beer halls that serve typical Viennese sausages with a jar of beer, restaurants that serve all kinds of foods, stores, meadows and woods where to go for a peaceful stroll. A train —the Liliput— takes visitors on a four-kilometre route through the main landmarks of this popular park.

THE PRATER'S WHEEL.

chönbrunn, the summer residence of the Hapsburg, is located on an old estate with large forests that Emperor Maximilian II bought in 1569 and transformed into a hunting reserve. It was in 1612 when Emperor Matthias "discovered" during a hunting outing the pretty fountain (schönen Brunnen) after which the estate was named. But Schönbrunn owes its fame to Leonor de Gonzaga, the wife of Ferdinand II, who in 1642 rebuilt the estate's main house to transform it into a summer retreat that hosted fantastic parties. Destroyed by the Turks during the 1683 siege of Vienna, it was another emperor, Leopold I, who commissioned the best known architect of his times, Johann Bernhard Fischer von Erlach, to build a palatial residence that had to be more lavish and larger than the Versailles Palace, an enterprise that was never fulfilled. The building works started in 1696 and four years later the building's main wing opened its doors. It would be here where Joseph I, Leopold's successor, would establish his residence. From 1711 the project stalled for several years due to the lack of interest showed in it by the new Emperor Charles VI. It was Empress Maria Theresa, who decided to turn Schönbrunn into her summer residence and the epicentre of court life, who gave the project the necessary momentum for its completion. In 1744, she commissioned architect Nikolaus von Pacassi to complete the building works. Around 1765 architect Johann Ferdinand Hetzendorf von

GARDENS AND SOUTHERN FAÇADE OF THE SCHÖNBRUNN PALACE.

FOUNTAIN OF THE HONOUR COURTYARD
AND THE PALACE'S MAIN FAÇADE.

Hohenberg, a representative of the classicist current of the time, took over. He is responsible for the roundabout at the heart of the park. Its last great refurbishment dates from 1819, when Johann Aman managed to unify the façade, which, following the custom distinguishing official Hapsburg buildings until the 20th century, was painted yellow.

The Schönbrunn Palace is said to be an illustration of the good taste and sensitivity of Empress Maria

ORANGE TREE GARDEN AND
THE EASTERN WING OF THE PALACE.

Theresa. Mother of 16 children, only 10 of whom lived to an adult age, she got personally involved in the choice of many of the palace's decorative elements. Perhaps because of her desire to strike a balance between her role as the head of state with that of mother, the residence is large but at the same time comfortable and cosy. This duality apparently led the Prussian ambassador to tell his king that it was more a family house than a royal palace. With a surface area of 1.76 square kilometres –four times larger than the Vatican– Schönbrunn has 1,441 rooms, including bedrooms and halls that could house the 1,500 people that formed part of the court during the summer months. Aside from Maria Theresa, her husband Franz and her children, the palace was also used by other members of the Hapsburg dynasty. Here lived and died, for instance, the Duke of Reichstadt, son of Napoleon and Marie Louise. The French emperor himself used the palace during the occupations of Vienna of 1805 and 1809. Another illustrious member of the Hapsburg dynasty, Emperor Franz Joseph I, had strong ties to Schönbrunn. He was born here in 1830 and died in the palace in 1916.

Between 1945 and 1947, the palace became the General Headquarters for the British occupation troops. In 1952 a new refurbishment restored the palace's past splendour following the destruction caused by the bombings of World War Second. Currently, the Schönbrunn is used for official events organised by the Austrian government.

The **palace park** follows a French design and stretches over 197 hectares. On its wide avenues flanked with 12-meter-high hedges, stand the **Orange Tree Greenhouse (Orangerie),** the **Chamber Garden (Kammergarten)**

VIEW OF THE GARDENS: NEPTUNE FOUNTAIN AND THE ROUNDABOUT.

PORTRAITS OF EMPRESS MARIA THERESA AND EMPEROR FRANZ I.

and the **Crown Prince Garden (Kronprinzengarten)**. Later, and with the goal of breaking up the strict symmetry of the design, new rococo elements were added to it, including the **Cascade of the Obelisk (Obeliskenkaskade)**, the **Neptune Fountain (Neptunbrunnen)**, the **Roman Ruins (Römische Ruine)** and the **Roundabout (Gloriette)**. The latter, through its 19 meter tall and 95 meter wide portico offers a beautiful view of the palace and the park. The **interior** of the palace is in line with the ostentatious style of the Hapsburg, displaying numerous Baroque and rococo ornaments. There is no lack either of decorative objects imported from different corners of the world, such as the china from the Far East. Among the most striking rooms is Franz Joseph and Sissi's joint bedroom, decorated in blue and white tones and with palisandro wood furniture, the Mirrors Room, where a very young Mozart —he was just six at the time— dazzled Maria Theresa during his first concert, and the Ceremonies Room, displaying several paintings depicting scenes from the history of the imperial court, including a portrait of Maria Theresa donning a dress made out of Brabante lace. Not less interesting are the Great Gallery, which is 40 meters long and 10 meters wide and that, with its sumptuous lamps, served as a ballroom for different events of the court; the Small Gallery, used for family celebrations; the Vieux-Laque Hall, decorated by Maria Theresa with lacquered panels from Beijing; Napoleon's bedroom, where his son the Duke of Reichstadt died from tuberculosis at age 21; the Hall of the Millions, one of the most valuable in the palace due to the small, Indo-Persian medallions embedded on the walls; the room with the imperial bed, which is where Franz Joseph I was born on August 18, 1830; the bedroom of Marie Antoinette, Maria Theresa's youngest daughter, who would become queen of France; and Franz Joseph's office, where the emperor started working every day at five in the morning.

THE BEDROOM OF FRANZ JOSÉ AND ELIZABETH.

THE MIRRORS' HALL AND THE VIEUX-LAQUE HALL.

HALL OF THE MILLIONS.

On the spot that once housed the winter riding school of Schönbrunn, stands since 1922 the **Wagon Museum (Wagenburg)**. With over 130 vehicles, including crowning, funerary, hunting and travel carriages, as well as sledges, berths and even several children's carriages, this is the world's largest collection of wagons. The jewel of the crown is the Imperial Carriage of the Viennese court, designed

CARRIAGE MUSEUM.

PALM TREE HOUSE.

for Franz I, Maria Theresa's husband, and that was drawn by eight horses.

Another of the palace's most outstanding buildings is the **Palm Tree House (Palmenhaus).** Built in 1883 out of steel and glass, it is the world's largest greenhouse of its kind, with three different halls that recreate different climatic conditions. When speaking of Schönbrunn, however, it is essential to mention the **Palace Theatre (Schlosstheater)** and the **Zoo (Tiergarten).** Built under request of Maria Theresa herself for the

PALACE THEATRE.

family's entertainment, the Palace Theatre is the oldest among Vienna's Baroque theatres and, interestingly enough, the only one still standing. In it were staged dozens of plays in tribute to the empress, including "The Businessman", directed by Mozart himself. From an octagonal pavilion that is now a café, Maria Theresa and her husband Franz used to observe the wild animals of their private zoo, which was built in 1752. Considered one of the oldest and most beautiful in the world, the zoo still today captivates with its collection of animals the thousands of visitors that cross its doors every year.

ZOO: OCTAGONAL PAVILION AND PENGUINS.

AUGARTEN PARK.

boarding school housing the Vienna's Boys' Choir. This famous choir, one of the city's cultural landmarks, was founded by Emperor Maximilian in 1498 and is formed by 96 children who sing donning their trademark sailors suits. Another Vienna landmark is located in the park: The **China Factory**, which is over 300 years old. Also noteworthy in the Augarten are two aerial defence towers that withstood the World War Second combats as well as all other later attempts to tear them down.

DECORATED PLATES THAT USED TO FORM PART OF THE COURT'S SILVERWARE AND CHINA COLLECTION. VIENNA'S CHINA FACTORY.

Having opened to the public in 1775 under orders of Joseph II, the Augarten Park is one of the oldest in Vienna. Occupying part of the grounds of an old imperial hunting palace, it is also known as The Favorite and its layout is based on that of the Aranjuez gardens in Madrid. Close to the main entrance is the **Augarten Palace**, which since 1948 is the main building of the

VIENNA'S BOYS' CHOIR.

THE ALTE DONAU OFFERS VISITORS DIFFERENT KINDS OF SERENE AQUATIC ACTIVITIES.

The attempts to divert the capricious Danube River (Donau) as it crosses Vienna date back to the late 19th century. When the works ended in 1988 the river had been divided into four sections: Alte Donau, Neue Donau, Donau and Donaukanal. One of the consequences of this new channelling was the creation of an artificial island, **Donauinsel.** With a length of 21 kilometres, it offers beaches, lush vegetation and several sporting and entertainment facilities. The transformation of the area also included the clean up of an old dump that would become the **Danube Park (Donaupark).** The best known site of the park is the **Danube Tower (Donauturm),** which is 250-meters-tall. Its viewpoint and its two gyrating restaurants, located 150 meters above the ground, offer spectacular panoramic views of the capital and its surroundings.

Nearby the tower is the **United Nations City (UNO-City)** or **Vienna International Centre-VIC.** Formed by three Y-shaped buildings, the compound was designed by architect Johann Staber and opened its doors in 1979. The willing disposition of the Austrian Government and the City Coun-

A LIGHTHOUSE OF DONAUINSEL (DANUBE ISLAND).

Boats along the Danube Canal, close to the Schwedenplatz, take visitors to nearby villages.

cil helped Vienna become the worldwide headquarters for four UN agencies, an honour it shares with New York, Geneva and Nairobi. At the Uno-City, which hosts among other institutions the International Atomic Energy Agency, work over 4,000 people from 100 different countries.

On the other bank of the river stands Vienna's tallest office building, the so-called **Millennium Tower**, a colossal and futuristic construction that rises 202 meters into the sky and was designed by architects Peichl, Podrecca Weber.

Danube Tower and modern pedestrian bridge over the Neue Donau.

THE VIEW FROM THE 150-METER-HIGH VIEWPOINT AT THE DANUBE TOWER, LOOKING TOWARD DONAU CITY (LEFT), THE DANUBE RIVER AND THE CITY.

THE NEUE DONAU, DONAU CITY AND UNO-CITY.

MILLENNIUM TOWER.

MOZART'S TOMB AT ST. MARK'S CEMETERY.

JOHANN STRAUSS' TOMB AT THE ZENTRALFRIEDHOF CEMETERY.

COURTYARD OF THE BEETHOVEN HOUSE KNOWN AS TESTAMENTHAUS, AS IT WAS HERE WHERE HE DRAFTED HIS WILL, AT 6, PROBUSGASSE (GRINZING).

Music has always played a very special part of everyday life in Vienna. The Hapsburg were said to be great musical connoisseurs and even that their sensitivity toward music was such that more than one emperor and empress became real virtuosos of different instruments. But the love for melody and harmony have never been exclusive of the Austrian capital's royalty and nobility. In general, all of Viennese society has helped make of this art one of the city's most outstanding features.

Vienna, as a fundamental musical hub, has been the birthplace of a wealth of great composers. The city has tried to keep alive the memory of all of them through different monuments and museums. Mozart (Salzburg 1756-Vienna 1791) is remembered, for instance, at Figarohaus, one of the 15 houses where the composer lived in Vienna and which is now open to the public; the Burggarten monument, erected in 1896; and his tomb in the St. Marks cemetery. Although he was buried in a common grave, the undertaker decided to place a simple tombstone with the composer's name on an empty tomb. Today the spot is visited by thousands of people every year. Beethoven (Bonn 1770-Vienna 1827) is believed to have moved houses at least 60 times. Currently open to the public are the houses of Eroica, Probusgasse and Schwarzspanier, where he died.

Other composers whose houses have been turned into museums include Franz Josef Haydn (Rohrau 1732-Vienna 1809), in Haydngasse; Franz Schubert (Vienna 1797-1828), in Nusdorfer Strasse; and Johann Strauss junior (Vienna 1825-1899), in Prater Strasse, where he composed his renowned "Blue Danube".

TECHNOLOGY MUSEUM.

Vienna is undoubtedly one of Europe's foremost cultural capitals, and it is also a city of museums. To those already mentioned we must add the **Technology Museum**, which displays James Watt's steam engine, the first car that used a fuel engine, Mitterhofers' typewriter and Josef Maderspergers' sewing machine. It also includes an appealing section devoted to old trains.

At the **Sigmund Freud Museum,** set up in the house where the founding father of psychoanalysis lived and worked from 1891 to 1938, visitors will find the virtually un-

SIGMUND FREUD MUSEUM.

changed waiting room to the doctor's office, several first editions of his publications, and personal objects.

Located in the Arsenal, the **Military Museum** stores several war objects as well as the blood-stained suit and the car in which Franz Ferdinand, heir to the Austro-Hungarian Empire and his wife Sofia were killed in Sarajevo on June 28, 1914.

The Liechtenstein palace houses the **Modern Art Museum**. Its collection includes works by Rubens, van Dyck, Lucas Cranach, Raphael, Rembrandt and Hamilton, as well as different collections of weapons, china and bronzes and a French ball carriage.

The wide-ranging number of museums in Vienna also includes institutions specialised in cinema and theatre, as well as a private museum that focuses exclusively on the film "The Third Man," shot in Vienna in 1948 and that premièred in London one year later.

ARMY MUSEUM.

ONE OF THE
GALLERIES AT THE
ARMY MUSEUM.

LIECHTENSTEIN
PALACE,
HEADQUARTERS OF
THE MODERN ART
MUSEUM.

KARL-MARX-HOF.

Built between 1927 and 1930 by architect Karl Ehn, a pupil of Otto Wagner, the Karl-Marx-Hof is Vienna's biggest and most renowned Gemeindebau or municipal residential building. The Gemeindebauen were council buildings financed by the City Hall during the so-called "red Vienna" period, which coincided with the first republic (1918-1934) following the victory of the Austrian Social Democrats in the municipal elections. Overall some 400 Gemeindebauen were erected, comprising some 64,000 apartments ranging from 30 to 60 square meters. The Karl-Marx-Hof is located in the Heiligenstadt quarter, in district 19 (Döbling), a previously marshy area that had to be dried up to urbanise it. With a façade of 1,100 meters, this is the longest single residential building in the world. It is divided into 1,300 apartments and common spaces such as parks, nurseries, a library, a small clinic and even a vegetable patch. Exhibiting some cubist elements, iron doors and small windows, the building's façades are decorated with references to Liberty, the Illustration, Social Security and Gymnastics. An inscription pays tribute to the political struggle of the working class of those years. "The first to do so in Europe, the Austrian workers opposed, on February 12, 1934, Fascism courageously. They fought for freedom, democracy and the republic".

For almost 100 years these four brick cubes built in 1896 stored the gas later supplied to the city of Vienna. After they fell out of use, in 1999 the City Council asked four prestigious architecture firms —Jean Nouvel, Coop Him-melb(l)au, Mangred Wehdorn and Wilhelm Holzbauer— to come up with different projects to re-convert and reopen these old Gasometers that have a diam-eter of 65 meters and are 75-meters-tall. The final result is an innovative set of housing units and offices joined by a large shopping centre.

THREE VIEWS OF THE GASOMETERS.

COBENZGASSE STREET AND THE PARISH CHURCH.

Considered today one more Vienna neighbourhood, Grinzing is the name of a village mentioned in a 1114 document as Ginzingan. Although it has a noteworthy church in late Gothic style and a quaint and pretty downtown, the area owes its current popularity to the Heurigen taverns, named after the young white and slightly fruity wine they serve.

ONE OF THE HOUSES WHERE BEETHOVEN LIVED IN GRINZING IS CURRENTLY A HEURIGEN TAVERN.

This wine is made out of grapes grown in the Grinzing vineyards, making Vienna perhaps the only capital in the world that can boast having its own, locally made wine within its municipal district.

VENUES WHERE THEY SERVE FOOD AND THE LOCAL HEURIGEN WINE.

Before actually having left the city, the terrain starts exhibiting a gradual slope that eventually leads to the first mountains of the Alps. Two hills, **Kahlenberg** and **Leopolds-berg**, offer on clear days good panoramic views of Vienna, with the Danube on the foreground, the Heurigen vineyards on one side and on the other the awe-inspiring **Kosterneuburg Abbey.** The abbey dates back to the rule of Leopold III of Babenberg, who in the early 12th century ordered the construction of a palace and a basilica that would later become an important cul-

KLOSTERNEUBURG ABBEY.

KLOSTERNEUBURG ABBEY.

tural centre. Around 1730, Charles VI, who had spent some years in Madrid, decided to transform the building into an El Escorial styled monastery, but the project was never finished. Nevertheless, the compound's beauty is astounding.

INSIDE THE KLOSTERNEUBURG ABBEY STANDS OUTS THE "VERDUN ALTAR." DATING FROM 1181 IT IS ONE OF THE MANY MARVELS VISITORS WILL HAVE A CHANCE TO ADMIRE IN THIS TEMPLE.

MAYERLING CASTLE.

The Austrian capital is surrounded by the so-called Vienna Woods. In the middle of this set of meadows and lush green woods stand out small villages and natural parks where the Viennese flock to on day trips. For instance there is **Lainzer Tiergarten,** a protected park that in the past formed part of the imperial hunting grounds; and **Mödling**, a quaint village with a pretty Renaissance Town Hall where Beethoven used to spend his summers. And there is also the **Mayerling Castle**, the stage of the tragic death

KREUZENSTEIN CASTLE.

CARNUNTUM: PAGANS DOOR.

of Archduke Rudolph, the only son of Franz Joseph I, who decided to kill himself together with his lover the Baroness Maria Vetsera.

There are other attractions such as the **Kreuzensteing Castle,** already mentioned in a 1115 document; the **Veste Liechtenstein Castle**, a true jewel of 12th century Romanesque; the **Heiligenkreuz Monastery**, also dating from the 12th century; the **Laxenburg Palace**, bought by the Hapsburg in the 14th century; and the **Carnuntum** archaeological site, showing the remains of the oldest Roman garrison in Austria.

In the village of Hinterbrühl is an old gypsum mine that had to be closed in 1912 after a badly planned and badly performed blast led to the flooding of its lower gallery. The **Seegrotte,** however, became after that Europe's largest underground lake. It is possible to visit its canals by boat in what makes an appealing day trip. In 1944 the cave was used by the Nazis to manufacture what would become the world's first jet combat planes.

THE SEEGROTTE.

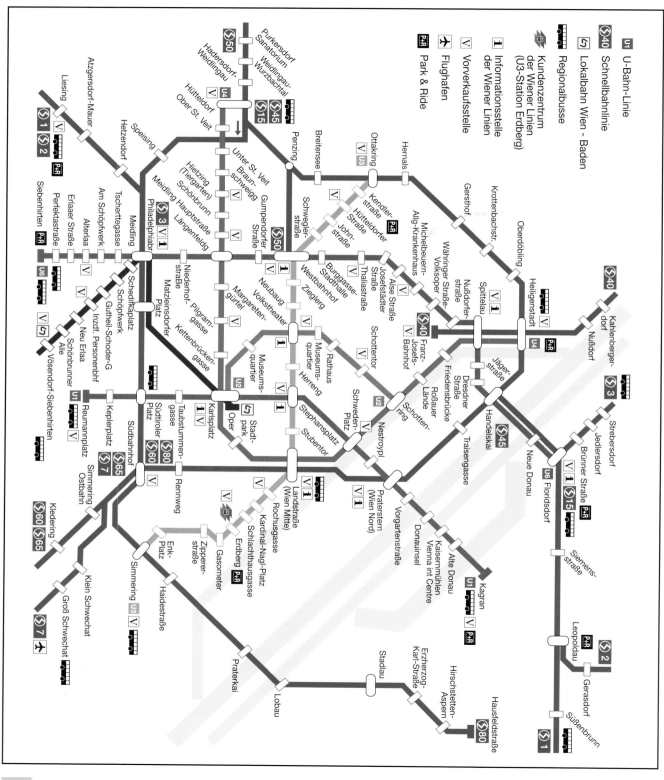

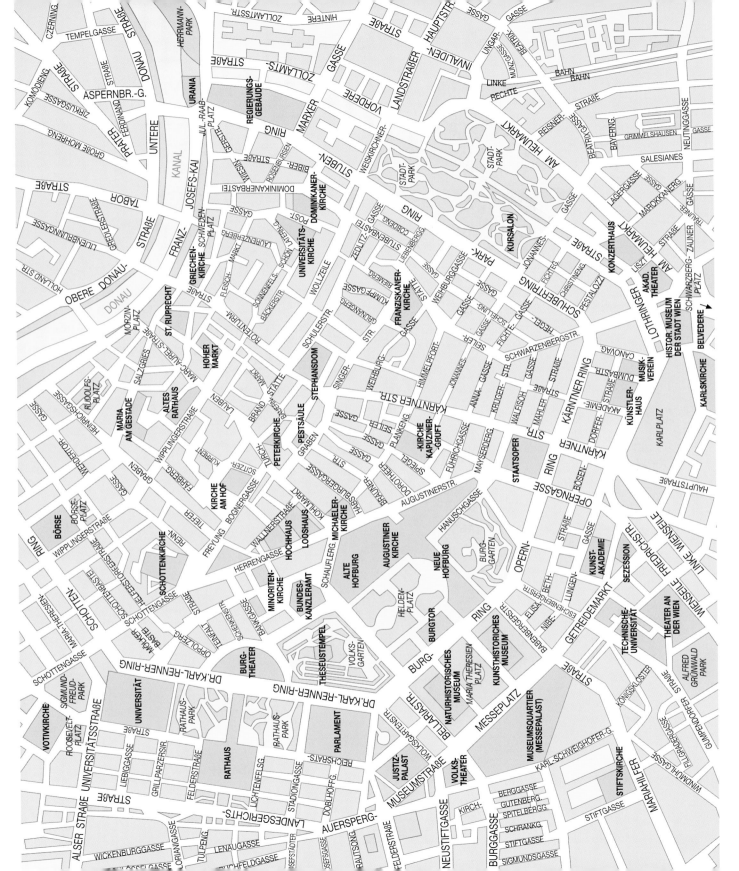

CONTENTS

EDITORIAL FISA ESCUDO DE ORO, S.A.
Tel: 93 230 86 00
www.eoro.com

I.S.B.N. 978-84-378-2739-1
Printed in Spain
Legal Dep. B. 17516-2007